I Died
Laughing

"But, seriously . . ."

Funeral Education with a Light Touch

Lisa Carlson

Upper Access, Inc.
PO Box 457 • 85 Upper Access Road
Hinesburg, VT 05461
E-mail info@upperaccess.com
Web http://www.upperaccess.com

I Died Laughing

Printed in the United States of America.

Upper Access Books
85 Upper Access Road
P.O. Box 457
Hinesburg, VT 05461
Business Phone: 802-482-2988 • Book Order Phone: 800-310-8320
E-mail *info@upperaccess.com* • Web *http://www.upperaccess.com*

Other books by Lisa Carlson:
Caring for Your Own Dead
Caring for the Dead: Your Final Act of Love

Cover by Betsy Lampe

At the request of the author and by arrangement with the publisher,
50% of the profits from the sale of this book will be donated to
Funeral Consumers Alliance.

Library of Congress Cataloging-in-Publication Data

Carlson, Lisa, 1938-
    I died laughing : funeral education with a light touch / Lisa Carlson.
        p. cm.
    Includes resources and index.
    ISBN 0-942679-25-3 (alk. paper)
    1. Death–Humor. 2. Funeral rites and ceremonies–Humor. I. Title.

PN6231.D35 C37 2001
306.9'02'07–dc21   00-049537

Contents

**Matters of Life
and Death
Inside**

Special Thanks

This book would not be the delightful and enjoyable tome it is without the generosity of the artists whose works embellish its pages. They have participated in this project in some cases with no charge, and in all other cases well below their customary fees. Those deserving special thanks include the following:

Estate of Edward Gorey
P.S. Mueller
Rina Piccolo
Sue Simon
James Alexander Thom
Joyce Tice

More Thanks & Resources

With a trip to the Library of Congress, one can verify that funeral humor has been around for many years. For example, *Bless Thee, Bully Doctor,* from which I've taken a couple of quotes, is dated 1883.

I am grateful to Kathy Walczak, librarian for the National Funeral Directors Association. She, too, has been collecting old and new material, including funeral humor, and graciously showed me through that collection. The trade journals such as *Funeral Monitor* and *Mortuary Law & Business Quarterly* have also provided gems from time to time.

Many of the jokes in this book I received via e-mail or telephone, and the original authors are unknown. I would appreciate knowing who they are, so that adequate credit may be given in the next printing.

Meanwhile, several authors were willing to collaborate, generously granting permission to quote from the following:

Memoirs of a Funeral Singer, unpublished, by Walter Boyden
The Road Less Graveled by Brent Holmes
Reincarnation by Wallace McRae
Last Words, Last Laughs by Richard Porteus
Twelve Step Program for the Dead by Terrel Templeman, Ph.D.
Women's Lip by Roz Warren

Brief quotes were also used from many other sources. Among them are:
Last Words of Famous Men compiled by Bega
Treasury of Humorous Quotations edited by Nicholas Bentley
The Art of Dying edited by F. Birrell and F. L. Lucas

871 Famous Last Words, and Put-downs, Insults, Squelches, Compliments, Rejoinders and Epigrams of Famous People by Gyles Brandreth
Solitude in Stone published by Clyde Chamberlin
Famous Last Words by Barnaby Conrad
Rubicon Dictionary by John Cook
Anguished English by Richard Lederer
Book of Blunders by David Macrea
Oxford Dictionary of Quotations
Kicking the Habit by Rina Piccolo

Some quotes appear in many sources—golden gems. It's hard to know who quoted first. Therefore, the speaker, not the publication, has been cited.

*Why a book on funeral humor?**

A couple of years ago, I was invited to give a talk on funeral planning at a large retirement home in nearby Burlington, Vermont. The woman who invited me seemed embarrassed that only a handful of people showed up. She apologized profusely, but I said I didn't mind. I proceeded to tell some jokes and to talk about funeral planning and the many choices that people may not realize they have. The next day, I got a call. Could I come back? The word had leaked out that besides learning a lot, they'd had fun, too.

We teach our children about money, politics, religion, and maybe sex. But we don't do a very good job teaching them about death, dying, and funerals. In the last few generations, we've lost the common lore of what to do at a time of death. When Grandma was laid out in the front parlor, everyone was involved, including the children.

One study by the National Hospice Foundation found that 75% of Americans haven't talked with their children about their final wishes. Is it because they don't know how? Would a good laugh break the ice?

---

* Although I refer to Funeral Consumers Alliance (FCA) throughout, this book is not a publication of FCA nor has it specifically been endorsed by FCA.

Ha·ha

From *The Awdrey-Gore Legacy*, © 1972 by Edward Gorey

Foreword

by John Abraham, D.D., Ph.D.**

Death is part of life. They go hand in glove.

Another essential part of life is humor. In the book *One Flew Over The Cuckoo's Nest* Randall Murphy, describing the asylum, said: "The first thing that got me about this place—there wasn't anybody laughing. I haven't heard a real laugh since I came through that door. Man, when you lose your laugh, you lose your footing."

The most common subjects of humor are the "unmentionables" such as sex and body waste. It's human nature to be somewhat uncomfortable in discussing these issues, so we joke about them. Death is another "unmentionable," often described with euphemisms. How many times have we heard that somebody has "expired," as if the person is a parking meter or driver's license? How many times following a death have you said, or heard others say, "I just don't know what to say." The fact is, even talking around the issue is better than no mention whatsoever.

Humor provides fellowship. People don't tell jokes to themselves, they tell them to others. Sharing humor about death is a reminder of our common mortality.

Humor can provide a safety valve for the release, relief, and discharge of tense emotion. I presided at a funeral where the family members experienced some confusion about who would be sitting where. They changed seats a couple of times, when someone in the group remarked, "Gee, here it is a funeral and we're playing musical chairs." The light-hearted comment helped to break the tension.

Mourning is the process by which the deceased goes from being a presence to a memory. Humor has the capacity to make that memory more indelible. Survivors remember and recall the silly, the foolish, the embarrassing moments and situations lived by the deceased. Recalling

---

**John Abraham is an Episcopal priest and thanatologist. For many years, he wrote a humor column for the Association for Death Education and Counseling newsletter.

them at a memorial gathering is not disrespectful of the dead person, but rather a reminder of the person's humanity, the things about the person that we enjoyed. The funny times are peak experiences, which stand out vividly and are endearingly remembered.

Yet another connection between comedy and death is that they are both great equalizers. There's the story of the deceased bank president, standing in line at the pearly gates, who asks if he can cut to the front of the line. St. Peter says "No, it doesn't matter how important you were on Earth, you have to wait in line like everybody else." A little later, a guy in green surgical scrubs goes right to the head of the line and through the gates. "What's the big idea?" the bank president asks. "How come the doctor could go right in?" St. Peter answers, "That's no doctor, that's God. He just likes to play doctor sometimes."

Humor can sometimes numb our emotions in a healthy, helpful way, by changing perceptions to make the circumstances seem less harsh. Take the story of the little boy whose cat died. The boy is bewildered, and asks over and over again why the cat had to die. The mother finally says, "Well, dear, God loved and wanted your cat." The boy looks at her and says, "What does God want with a dead cat?" With this turn of a phrase, only the perception is altered. The circumstances are the same. The cat is still dead, but we can laugh instead of cry.

There's a serious purpose to Lisa Carlson's book. It has a lot of useful information—things you should know if it's your responsibility to make funeral arrangements for a friend or relative, and things you should know in planning ahead for what will be done when you die. Nobody likes to ponder these issues at great length, which is why, so often, people are forced to make overly hasty decisions at a time of grief. The information here is made easy to digest because it is surrounded by humor.

Comedy is the world of energy going nowhere in particular, but enjoying the going. In the comic vision, life is like a dance. The purpose of dancing is not to get from Point A to Point B on the dance floor, it's the dancing itself. And the purpose of life is to live. With humor, we should strive for the same end. This book will have served its purpose if you laugh and enjoy the laughter.

Old age ain't no place for sissies

—*Bette Davis*

~ § ~

To me, old age is always 15 years older than I am.

—*Bernard Baruch*

Growing old is inevitable. Growing up is optional.

Sir Ernest Henry Shackleton to his doctor toward the end: "You are always wanting me to give up something. What do you want me to give up now?"

~ § ~

A 101-year-old patient went to the doctor with a complaint of pain in his left leg. The doctor's response was that pain was to be expected at his age. To this the patient responded, "Why doesn't my 101-year-old right leg hurt?"

~ § ~

Notes from a hospice journal: One patient identified his place of worship as "Scared Heart." Others listed diagnoses as: "cancer of the lover," "chorionic brian syndrome," and "cementia metal disorder."

~ § ~

From a Paris newspaper: Dr. X has been appointed head physician to the Hôspital de la Charité. Orders have been issued by the authorities for the immediate extension of the Cemetery de Parmasse.

~ § ~

The good die young—because they see it's no use living if you've got to be good.
—*John Barrymore*

~ § ~

I like my ability to forget.

[From a student paper:] A natural death is where you die by yourself without a doctor's help.

From a medical record: Healthy-appearing decrepit 69-year-old man, mentally alert but forgetful.

"Excuse me, but in taking the census it is necessary to get all the particulars. What did she die of?"

"Improvements."

"I beg your pardon, sir, but I don't think that I quite understand."

"Of improvements, sir; *improvements.*"

"Why, how can that be?"

"Well, the doctor come Monday night and said there was improvement. Tuesday morning he come and said there was some more improvements, and Tuesday night he said there was more improvements than there was before. Wednesday mornin' he said the improvements was continuin', and that night she died, and if she didn't die of improvements, then I don't know what ailed her."　　　　　　　　　　　　　　—From *Bless Thee, Bully Doctor*

~ § ~

Don't take life so seriously. It's not permanent.

~ § ~

The art of medicine consists of amusing the patient while nature cures the disease.　　　　　　　　　　　　　　　　　　—*Voltaire*

~ § ~

We all labour against our own cure, for death is the cure of all diseases.　　　　　　　　　　　　　　　　　　—*Sir Thomas Brown*

~ § ~

Medicine is the only profession that labours incessantly to destroy the reason for its own existence.　　　　　　　　　　—*James Bryce*

Death is just a distant rumor to the young.

—*Andy Rooney*

~ § ~

I am dying with the help of too many physicians.

—*Alexander the Great*

~ § ~

Die, my dear doctor? That is the last thing I shall do.

—*Viscount Palmerston*

~ § ~

Grandfather had been complaining about his treatment at the nursing home, so Bobby thought he would check it out. On his next visit, the grandson quietly observed from the back of the day room as the residents were watching TV. As his grandfather started to lean to the right, an aide rushed over and straightened him up. A few minutes later, Grandfather started listing to the left. Again the aide rushed over and straightened him up.

Finally, Bobby went over to greet his grandfather. "Gramps, I've been watching. You seem to be getting excellent care here."

"Excellent care? Hell, you can't even fart around here."

~ § ~

I have firmly decided to bite the dust with a minimum of medical assistance when my time comes, and up to then to sin to my wicked heart's content.

—*Albert Einstein*

~ § ~

"Sam, I'm sorry to say, but you've got only six months to live."

"Doc, I think I want a second opinion."

"Okay, Sam, you're ugly."

From *The Gashlycrumb Tinies*, © 1963 by Edward Gorey

F is for FANNY sucked dry by a leech

Anything awful makes me laugh. I misbehaved once at a funeral.
—*Charles Lamb*

~ § ~

Heard at lunch with a very wealthy funeral chain operator:
"Hospitals are my warehouse."

~ § ~

When you are ill, make haste to forgive your enemies, for you may recover.
—*Ambrose Bierce*

~ § ~

Don't let it end like this. Tell them I said something.
—Pancho Villa, on his deathbed

Mrs. Murphy and Mrs. Cohen lived next door to each other for over 40 years and became loving friends. One day, Mrs. Murphy said to Mrs. Cohen, "Our houses are becoming too much for us. Let's sell them and move into a retirement home."

With long waiting lists, Mrs. Cohen took the first vacancy—at a Jewish home. Mrs. Murphy finally went to live at a Catholic place.

But Mrs. Murphy felt very lonesome for Mrs. Cohen. One day she asked to be driven over to visit her old friend. When she arrived, she was greeted with open arms, hugs and kisses. "So how do you like it here?" Mrs. Murphy asked.

Mrs. Cohen went on and on about the wonderful food, the facility, and the caregivers. Then she said, "You know, the best thing is that I now have a boyfriend."

"Isn't that wonderful. Tell me what you do," asked Mrs. Murphy.

"After lunch, we go up to my room and sit on the bed. I let him touch me on top and then on the bottom, and then we sing Jewish songs." Mrs. Cohen went on, "And how is it with you?"

Mrs. Murphy said it was also wonderful at her new facility and that she, too, had a boyfriend.

"So what do you do?" asked Mrs. Cohen.

"We also go up to my room after lunch," said Mrs. Murphy, "I let him touch me on top and then I let him touch me down below."

"And then what?" asked Mrs. Cohen. Said Mrs. Murphy, "Since we don't know any Jewish songs, we make love."

Worried woman: "Since we just moved here, I don't know anything about this hospital."

Neighbor: "Don't worry. The doctors and nurses are excellent. I should know—this is where my husband died."

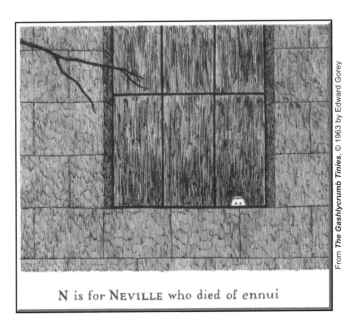

N is for NEVILLE who died of ennui

From *The Gashlycrumb Tinies*, © 1963 by Edward Gorey

Doctor, as I believe you would not choose to tell anything but the truth, you had better say that I am dying as fast as my enemies (if I have any) could wish, and as easily and cheerfully as my friends could desire.
                                                                        —*Hume*

~ § ~

Doctor's note on the chart of a patient who died: Patient failed to fulfill his wellness potential.

~ § ~

Ben Franklin, in response to a friend wishing him to get well soon: "I hope not."

A woman accompanied her husband to the doctor's office. After his check-up, the doctor called the wife into his office alone. He said, "Your husband is suffering from a very severe disease combined with horrible stress. If you don't do the following, your husband will surely die:

Each morning, fix him a healthy breakfast. Be pleasant and make sure he is in a good mood.

For lunch make him a nutritious meal he can take to work. And for dinner, prepare an especially nice meal for him.

Don't burden him with chores, as this could further his stress.

Don't discuss your problems with him; it will only make his stress worse.

Try to relax your husband in the evening by wearing lingerie and giving him plenty of back rubs.

Encourage him to watch some type of team sporting event on television.

And, most importantly, make love with your husband several times a week and satisfy his every whim.

And if you can do this for the next 10 months to a year, I think your husband will regain his health completely."

On the way home, the husband asked his wife, "What did the doctor say?"

"You're going to die," she replied.

~ § ~

Ask her to wait a moment—I am almost done.

—Carl Friedrich Gauss, while working, when informed that his wife was dying

~ *I Died Laughing* ~

The woman's husband had been slipping in and out of a coma for several months, yet she stayed by his bedside every single day. One day, when he came to, he motioned for her to come nearer. As she sat by him, he whispered, eyes full of tears, "You know what? You have been with me all through the bad times. When I got fired, you were there to support me. When my business failed, you were there. When I got shot, you were by my side. When we lost the house, you stayed right there. When my health started failing, you were still by my side. . . . You know what?"

"What, dear?" she gently asked, smiling as her heart began to fill with warmth.

"I think you're bad luck."

Z is for ZILLAH who drank too much gin

~ *I Died Laughing* ~

For many years, Mildred wouldn't marry Clyde because she had to take care of her parents. Finally, having lived into their 90s, both parents had passed away. By this time, Mildred and Clyde were in their 70s, but at last they were free to marry.

Coming from a generation that didn't believe in hanky-panky outside marriage, Clyde looked forward eagerly to their wedding night. He could tell that Mildred was nervous and vowed to himself to be tender and gentle.

As she sat on the edge of the bed in her flannel nightie nervously wringing her hands, Clyde decided to make the first move. He reached over and slipped the nightie off one shoulder. To his dismay, he saw that her breast was wrinkled and sagging, not at all like the pin-up pictures in the men's room at the local gas station.

Mildred, now more nervous than ever, finally mustered her courage. "Clyde, I have to tell you. . . . I have acute angina."
"That's good," he said, "because the rest of you hasn't weathered too well."

~ § ~

There's lots of bed-hopping at the nursing homes . . .
Everyone's looking for a dry place to sleep.

~ § ~

May my last breath be drawn through a pipe and exhaled in a pun.
—*Charles Lamb*

An old man at a nursing home shuffled up the hall to the nurses' station and said, "My penis is dead."

The nurse replied sympathetically, "Ohhhhh, that's too bad. But that does happen sometimes." And she sent him back to his room.

A little while later, the old man shuffled up the hall again, this time with his penis hanging out of his pajamas. The nurse looked at him and said, "I thought you said your penis died."

"It did," he replied, "this is the viewing."

"Smoking or Non-Smoking?"

To someone who commented that she couldn't get to heaven with smoke on her breath: "Yes, chile, but when I goes to heaven I expect to leave my breath behind."
—*Sojourner Truth*

Photo © 1999 by Sue Simon.

The two old ladies wheeled their walkers outside the nursing home to have a smoke. Shortly, it began to rain. Margaret fumbled in her purse and pulled out a condom, snipped the end off, slipped it over her cigarette, and kept on puffing.

"Why," said Helen, "I've never seen a raincoat for a cigarette before."

"This isn't a raincoat," snapped Margaret. "It's a condom. Buy 'em at any drug store."

Whatever you call it, Helen was impressed. So she shuffled off to the drugstore the next day. "I'd like a package of condoms," she told the clerk.

A little flustered, the clerk finally blurted, "What brand?"

"Oh, it doesn't matter as long as it fits a Camel," piped Helen.

But seriously . . .

The Robert Wood Johnson Foundation spent $27 million, only to learn that medical people were NOT honoring Living Wills unless there was an aggressive family member who intervened.

Lesson: Make sure the person you name as your health-care agent is a tough dude or a witch-on-wheels.

Advance Directives include:
    Living Will
    Comfort care request
    Do-not-resuscitate order
    Medical power of attorney
    Financial power of attorney
    Agent for body disposition
    Funeral or memorial plans
    Your own cremation authorization

If you don't put your wishes in writing, there's no way to prove how you want to be treated toward the end of your life and after.

Copies of your "Advance Directives" should be filed with your hospital records and given to:
    your doctor, *and*
    your retirement home staff, *or*
    your nursing home staff, *and*
    all next-of-kin and/or life partner, *and*
    any others who will be caring for you.

Keep your own copies in a pouch in the freezer. Make sure others know the pouch is there if you have not distributed copies. It's a good idea to have an extra set to carry while traveling.

Funeral Consumers Alliance has a "Before I Go, You Should Know" end-of-life planning kit with state-specific advance directives. It comes in a plastic document pouch with a magnet for the refrigerator door ($10). To order, call 800-765-0107.

Next-of-kin is usually determined in the following order:
> Spouse
> Adult children—all or a majority
> Parents
> Adult siblings . . . and so on

Unless you live in a state that provides for a designated agent for body disposition or that will honor your written wishes after you die, your next-of-kin will be responsible for making funeral decisions. This is true even if the person has been estranged from you. In a few states, the choice of cremation can be vetoed by next-of-kin. Be sure to find out what your rights are in your state.

If death is an expected one, DO NOT call 911. Instead, call the attending doctor or nurse. Then call the funeral home if you are using one.

Here Today, Gone Tomorrow

[From a student paper:] Oftentimes it's fatal to live too long.

~ § ~

A preacher went to his church office on Monday morning and discovered a dead jackass (mule) in the churchyard. He called the police. Since there did not appear to be any foul play, the police referred the preacher to the health department.

They said since there was no health threat, he should call the sanitation department. The sanitation manager said he could not pick up the mule without authorization from the mayor.

The preacher knew the mayor, and was not eager to call him. The mayor had a bad temper and was generally hard to deal with, but the preacher, seeing no alternative, made the call.

The mayor, as expected, immediately began to rant and rave at the pastor and finally said, "Why did you call me anyway? Isn't it your job to bury the dead?"

The preacher paused for a brief prayer and asked the Lord to direct his response. He was led to say, "Yes, Mayor, it is my job to bury the dead, but I always like to notify the next-of-kin first."

~ § ~

Don't knock on death's door:
Ring the bell and run—
He hates that.

~ § ~

It is amazing how nice people are to you when they know you are going away.

—*Arlen*

NEAR DEATH EXPERIENCE.

BUS

From *Shrink Wrap*, © 1992 by P.S. Mueller

"This wall-paper is terrible. One of us has to go."

—*Oscar Wilde*

~ § ~

[From a list of quotations attributed to children:] "I believe you should live each day as if it were your last, which is why I don't have any clean laundry. Come on, who wants to wash clothes on the last day of their life?"

~ § ~

Last words are for fools who haven't said enough.

—*Karl Marx*

~ § ~

Biography is one of the new terrors of death.

—*John Arbuthnot*

O'Malley walked back into the waiting room where his son was. "Well, son, we celebrate when things are good, and we celebrate when things don't go so well. In this case things aren't so well. I have cancer and just a short time to live. Let's head for the pub and have a few pints."

After three or four pints, the two were feeling a little less somber. There were some laughs and more beers. O'Malley's old friends finally asked what the two were celebrating. "I've been diagnosed with AIDS. Got only a few weeks to live." The friends gave their condolences, and they had a couple more beers.

After his friends had left, O'Malley's son leaned over and whispered, "Dad, I thought you were dying from cancer! You just told your friends you were dying from AIDS."

"I am dying of cancer, son. I just don't want any of them sleeping with your mother after I'm gone."

From *The Osbick Bird* © 1970 by Edward Gorey

~ I Died Laughing ~

Funeral director to customer:
"Let me tell you about my lay-away plan."

~ § ~

One preneed salesman didn't want to take "no" for an answer and wouldn't leave. In complete annoyance, the spry senior got up, went to her bedroom, and let out her pet iguana. The salesman didn't even wait to put on his shoes and fled with them under his arm.
—*Described in e-mail from an FCA member*

~ § ~

Not only is there a skeleton in every closet, but there is a screw loose in every skeleton.
—*Samuel Butler*

The sooner you die, the more you save on living expenses.

~ § ~

He died penniless. Sounds like good timing to me.

~ § ~

If you have intercourse, you run the risk of dying and the
ramifications of death are final.
—*Cyndi Lauper*

Sign on a Spanish airline: Bags to be used in case of sickness or to gather remains.

~ § ~

FINAL EXIT, the suicide how-to book, was a best-seller for 19 weeks after its publication. One year later, the paperback version came out and did a brisk business. Who waited for the paperback and what did the cheapskates do with their savings?

—*Meredith Anthony & Alison Power*

~ § ~

A well-known orchestra conductor died, but his agency continued to receive phone calls for him some months after his death. In each instance, the caller was gently informed that the maestro had died. Finally, the receptionist realized it was the same voice calling each time. "Why do you continue to call, when I've told you he has passed away?" she asked. The caller hesitated and then replied, "I used to be a member of his orchestra, and I can't tell you how much it cheers me to hear you say he is gone."

~ § ~

They say you shouldn't say nothing about the dead unless it's good. He's dead. Good.

—*Moms Mabley*

Cancel my subscription to "Healthy Living."

DEATH CERTIFICATES

[From a doctor:] The most common metaphor I hear clinicians use when speaking to nonmedical personnel and families is "lost." "We *lost* the patient," or "We attempted resuscitation but we *lost* him anyway." When I first came to this country, this struck me as rather odd. I wanted to say, "Well, we didn't really lose your husband. We know where he is, it's just he's not breathing any more."

~ § ~

It's time I were gone, since I keep so many waiting.
—*Dauphin of France (on his deathbed)*

My cousin died. He was a dyslexic policeman who had a heart attack. They found him by the phone trying to dial 119.

—Joan Rivers

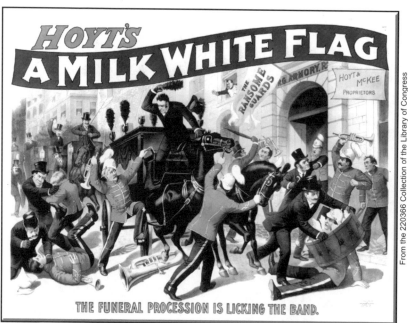

James Cross, Scottish physicist, after a life of abstention, asked for spirits on his deathbed: "I'll take a wee drop of that. I don't think there's much fear of me learning to drink now."

~ § ~

Ballerina Anna Pavlova on her deathbed: "Get my swan costume ready."

~ § ~

Death: to stop sinning suddenly.

—E. Hubbard

I dreamed I went to Heaven in my Maidenform Bra.

~ § ~

Everything comes to him who waits—among other things, death.
—*Francis Bradley*

~ § ~

[In response to an invitation:] I must ask to be excused, as I have to die. —*Goethe's mother*

~ § ~

I'm not afraid to die. I just don't want to be there when it happens. —*Woody Allen*

~ § ~

Let us endeavor so to live that when we come to die, even the undertaker will be sorry. —*Mark Twain*

~ § ~

When told on his deathbed that the angels were waiting, Ethan Allen replied, "Waiting are they? Waiting are they? Well, God-damn 'em, let 'em wait."

If this is dying, I don't think much of it.   *—Lytton Strachey*

~ § ~

Dying is a very dull, dreary affair. And my advice to you is to have nothing whatever to do with it.   *—Somerset Maugham*

~ § ~

Life is a jest, and all things show it.
I thought so once, and now I know it.
    —John Gay

~ § ~

Well, doc. I guess this is the main event.
    —Wilson Mizner, on his deathbed

About the Zote what can be said?
There was just one, and now it's dead.

From *The Utter Zoo Alphabet*, © 1998 by Edward Gorey

33

"Ah, Thomas, who's dead?"

"Old Slocum."

"Ah! What complaint?"

"There's no complaint—everybody's satisfied."

Illustration from *Bless Thee, Bully Doctor*

Two ditch diggers were repairing some roadside damage directly across the street from a house of ill repute when they witnessed a Protestant Reverend lurking about and then ducking into the house. "Would ye look at that, Darby!" said Paddy. "What a shameful disgrace, those Protestant Reverends sinning in a house the likes of that place!" They both shook their heads in disgust and continued their work.

A short time later they watched as a Rabbi looked around himself cautiously and then darted into the house when he was satisfied no one had spied him. "Did ye see that, Darby?" Paddy asked in shock and disbelief. "Is nothing holy any more? I just can't understand what the world is coming to these days. A man of the cloth indulging himself in sins of the flesh. 'Tis a shame, I tell ya!"

A little while later they saw a third man, a Catholic Priest, lurking about the house looking around to see if any one was watching, and then quietly sneaking in the door. "Oh no, Darby, look!" said Paddy, removing his cap. "One of the poor girls musta died."

An insurance company congratulated its shareholders on the "low rate of morality during the past year."

A lawyer is a learned gentleman who rescues your estate from your enemies and keeps it for himself.
—*Henry Brougham*

Never go to a doctor whose office plants have died.

—*Erma Bombeck*

~ § ~

I believe that people would be alive today if there were a death penalty.

—*Nancy Reagan*

~ § ~

William Palmer, hanged for poisoning a friend, stepping onto the gallows trap: "Are you sure it's safe?"

~ § ~

Three little boys were gathered around their grandfather on the porch. The oldest looked up at his grandfather and asked, "Grandpa, can you make a sound like a frog?" The grandfather looked down and said, "No I don't feel like making a sound like a frog today."

The next in age sitting by Grandpa on the porch swing said, "Oh, please, Grandpa. Make a sound like a frog. We really want to hear you sound like a frog." "Nope," said the grandfather, "I'm feeling kinda grumpy today and I don't want to make any frog sounds."

The youngest, sitting on Grandpa's lap, pleaded, "Oh, Grandpappy, if you would just make a little frog sound, I will give you oodles and oodles of hugs." Well, the grandfather was curious and asked, "Why do you boys want me to make a frog sound?" The youngest replied, "Cause Mommy said when you croak, we can all go to Disney World."

~ § ~

[From a news article:] Although the patient had never been fatally ill before, he woke up dead.

[From a student paper:] When you breathe, you inspire. When you do not breathe, you expire.

~ § ~

[Newspaper headline:] Smokers are productive, but death cuts efficiency.

~ § ~

[From a student paper:] In many states, murderers are put to death by electrolysis.

~ § ~

World Health Organization officials expressed disappointment at the group's finding that, despite the enormous efforts of doctors, rescue workers, and other medical professionals worldwide, the global death rate remains constant at 100 percent.　　*—the Onion*

So much for your get-well cards.

A Twelve-Step Program for the Dead*

by Terrel L. Templeman, Ph.D.

The *Journal of Polymorphous Perversity* was the first publication to address an often neglected though certainly grave topic in the field of psychotherapy, namely therapy of the dead. Mental health professionals have generally found this type of client most resistant to entering treatment.

My colleagues and I believe that we have a new approach to this lifeless field. We present here for the first time a 12-step program for the dead, which is modeled closely after other 12-step programs. Dead Ones Anonymous (DOA) groups allow the dead to meet in supportive settings to develop mutual trust and to realize that they are not alone in their dead pursuits. Most dead come from dysfunctional families, and we have encouraged DOA members to share their feelings about the burden of being unjustly maligned or irrationally revered by the living.

What Are the 12 Steps?

1. Accept the fact that you are dead. Stop fighting it. Remind yourself that death is simply nature's way of telling you to slow down.

2. Take responsibility for your own inertia. Stop blaming it on those around you. Remember, today is the first day of the rest of your death.

3. Give your burdens up to a higher power and don't try to play God. Recite the Serenity Prayer and pray for the wisdom to know the difference between life and death.

4. Take a holiday. In fact, take a vacation once in a while. Don't take death so seriously. Remember, you die only once.

5. Remind yourself that death is a disease. It begins the day you are

---

born, progresses until the day you die, and then takes over completely. For 10 out of every 10 people, this disease is fatal.

6. Admit that you are powerless over death. If you thought life was unmanageable, just try keeping all your loose ends together when you are dead!
7. Make a searching and fearless mortal inventory of yourself. See what you can find.
8. Humbly ask someone to see that your grave is kept clean.
9. Know that you are not alone in this affliction.
10. Remember that things could always be worse.
11. Relinquish materialism and let go of worldly possessions. Remember, you can't take it with you.
12. Strive for spiritual awakening as long as you are dead, and remember: It's never too late to try for heaven.

But Seriously . . .

Franklin Roosevelt left detailed instructions for his funeral, but he deposited them in his safe without informing anyone. Only after his funeral did his family realize that he explicitly rejected much of what had been done—the embalming, the use of an expensive casket, and the grave liner or vault. He desired a rapid return of his crippled body to the elements.   —*Cremation Concerns* by W. E. Phipps

It *always* pays to plan ahead. It *rarely* pays to pay ahead.

If you have prepaid for your funeral, you may not get all of your money back if—

- you die while traveling
- you move
- you change your mind from body burial to cremation
- you divorce or remarry and want to change plans
- you find another funeral home you like better or that's cheaper
- you need the money for an emergency now
- the funeral home goes out of business.

Prepaying for a funeral to "lock in prices" won't save you money if a lower-cost facility opens nearby next year, a trend that has started in many parts of the country.

If someone contacts you to sell you a funeral or cemetery plan, just say "NO." The sales person likely has a quota to meet this week, and the "specials" being offered may not be so special after all. It is better not to buy unless YOU have initiated the contact *and* have done some shopping around.

A funeral director may convert your prepaid trust account to "funeral insurance" without telling you, depending on the state in which you live. If that happens, the funeral director gets a commission, and the cash value (if you wanted to cancel) has been reduced. If you have to cash in the policy early, you'll get pennies on the dollar.

Another possible option is life insurance. However, keep in mind that Medicaid may consider life insurance to be an asset and require you to sell it prior to eligibility for medical benefits. Also, some funeral homes may charge a processing fee for accepting a life insurance policy. If it's 5% of a $5,000 bill—$250—that's a hefty chunk, like charging 60% interest a year, as most policies will pay up within 30 days. You'd be better off to borrow the money if you can, even using a high-interest credit card if necessary.

The Social Security death benefit is only $255, available to a surviving spouse or dependent children. For those without a surviving spouse or dependent children, there are no benefits.

Veterans, their spouses, and their dependent children are entitled to free burial space in a national cemetery. This will include the opening and closing, the vault (if required), and a marker. It is your responsibility to get the body or cremated remains to the cemetery.

Veterans only—not their spouses or children—are entitled to a free marker for a grave in any cemetery.

Although veterans are eligible for body burial at sea, it doesn't sound so romantic when you learn what's involved:

- embalming with a high degree of preservation—"stiff," in case the casket has to sit on the dock for 60 days
- 150 lbs. of extra weight
- a metal casket with 20 two-inch holes and six plastic straps.

An alternative to burial at sea in a casket is having your ashes scattered in the ocean. The Navy provides this service to veterans free of charge. This is a more ecological alternative to leaving a rusting casket on the ocean floor.

For more information on veterans' funeral and burial benefits, call 800-827-1000. That will ring in the regional VA office for the state from which you called.

From *Shrink Wrap*, © 1992 by P.S. Mueller

Much Adieu about Nothing

Funeral, *n.* A pageant whereby we attest our respect for the dead by enriching the undertaker, and strengthen our grief by an expenditure that deepens our groans and doubles our tears.

—*Ambrose Bierce*

~ § ~

Funeral pomp is more for the vanity of the living than for the honor of the dead.

—*François, Duc de la Rochefoucauld*

~ § ~

I have been to a funeral; I can't describe to you the howl which the widow set up at proper intervals.

—*Charles Lamb*

~ § ~

Animals have these advantages over man: They have no theologians to instruct them, their funerals cost them nothing, and no one starts lawsuits over their wills.

—*Voltaire*

~ § ~

A wedding is just like a funeral except that you get to smell your own flowers.

—*Grace Hansen*

~ § ~

They say such nice things about people at their funerals that it makes me sad to realize that I'm going to miss mine by just a few days.

—*Garrison Keillor*

Will your obituary appear in the *New York Times?*

Guaranteed:

Presidents
First doctor to transplant a heart
Winners of a Nobel Prize
Outstanding artists
Superstars in entertainment
Captains of finance or industry
Royalty
Infamous criminals, scoundrels

Forget it (buy a death notice):

Small-time politicians
Petty thieves
Mediocre artists
Bank tellers
Computer programmers
Housewives
State police
Insurance salesmen

Maybe:

Famous chefs
Authors of best sellers
Opera divas
Murky poets
Judges
College presidents and professors
Former Nazis who have cleansed themselves by building weaponry for the United States
Former communists who have purged themselves to the FBI
Sports personalities
Movie, radio, television figures
Generals and admirals
Philanthropists
Certified oddballs: Flagpole sitters, bosom friends of multiple cats and dogs, recluses, marathon dancers
Abrasive controversial figures
—*Alden Whitman*

The American Way of Death*

The editor of a French magazine had read of an American "funeral cosmetics company" and presumed it to be the only one in the world. (Make-up on a corpse would generally be considered ludicrous in European countries.) An unusual story, he thought, and assigned a Reuters' writer to check it out.

The writer soon found that it didn't stop with cosmetics or one company. There were lots of companies, providing not only cosmetics but burial footwear and burial clothing, too. "But I guess those are just good quality things in the latest styles," she suggested.

"Not exactly . . ." I described the slit in the back so one didn't have to wrestle the whole body into a dress or suit—just drape and tuck. And of course I shared Jessica Mitford's fascination with the "Fit-a-fut" oxfords from "Practical Footware."

By this time we were both giggling. "What else is there?" the writer asked. "Well, let me check," and I got out my *Blue Book of Funeral Directors,* turning to the "Buyer's Guide" section in the back. "There are 12 companies under 'Cosmetics'," I offered. "Do you have them all?" Then my eye caught a display ad. "Get this. 'Try Nadene Cover-Up Cosmetics and discover what over 7,000 other funeral directors already know. 100% GUARANTEED. ABSOLUTELY RISK FREE'."

"Absolutely risk free to whom?" she asked in charged disbelief. And the mirth rolled back and forth again on the phone lines. We're only in the "C" section, and already this has been the high point of my week on the laughter scale. When we got to the "H" section, it happened again: there was "Hosiery." With the bottom half of the casket often closed even with an open-casket affair, who's buying enough funeral hosiery to induce eight companies to list their names here? (If there's a choice among "ecru," "taupe," or "support hose," which one do you pick? Knee-highs? Or do they offer panty-hose? Something to go with the "Fit-a-fut" oxfords?)

But the clincher that had us both leaking tears of laughter as we gave in to all-too-vivid imaginations came in the "U" section: "Underwear"—Six funeral clothing companies presumably paid extra for these listings. "Was he a boxer man or did he prefer briefs?" she croaked in funereal concern, gasping between attacks of laughter at the American way of death.

---

* From *Caring for the Dead: Your Final Act of Love,* Upper Access, 1998. Also posted on the Funeral Consumers Alliance Web site.

From an actual trade brochure describing a 4½" white plastic screw:

A/V Closure Device
"To provide funeral service professionals with an efficient, cost effective product that will close the anal and vaginal orifices while preserving the dignity of the deceased."

~ § ~

Widow to funeral director as she questioned some of the charges:
"Why embalming?"
"He won't last."
"Well, he didn't last. That's why he's here."

~ § ~

About her fitness instructor:
"The trainer works me harder than a funeral-home fan in July."
—*Former Texas governor Ann Richards*

~ § ~

She looks better than she did when she was alive.

~ § ~

It's better to be seen than viewed.

~ § ~

Remember that always dressing in understated good taste is the same as playing dead.
—*Susan Catherine*

~ I Died Laughing ~

As Dave Barry might say, "We are not making this up." From the study guide for the national funeral directors exam: Which of the following is NOT one of the pigment cosmetics necessary to match all skin colors?

   A. Red
   B. Brown
   C. Green
   D. Yellow

~ § ~

It's astonishing what people throughout history have done to the bodies of their dead. They've bandaged them in linen, salted them down like halibut, packed them in quicklime, pumped them full of preservatives, mounted them on ships' bows, left them to wither in tree houses, baked them, smoked them, painted them, and interred them variously. Each for specific reasons detailed in their mythologies.

~ § ~

A woman goes to the newspaper office to arrange the obituary for her recently deceased husband. The editor tells her that the price is 50 cents per word. She says "Let it read 'Fred Brown Died'."

The editor informs her that there is a seven-word minimum. She thinks a moment and says, "In that case, let it read 'Fred Brown Died—1988 pickup for sale'."

Available for Show and Tell

I'm not afraid of death. It's the make-over at the undertaker's that scares me. They try to make you look as lifelike as possible, which defeats the whole purpose. It's hard to feel bad for somebody who looks better than you do.
—*Anita Wise*

~ § ~

A lot of damned foolery.
—*Oliver Wendell Holmes*

~ § ~

Interesting language from funeral home price lists:

Emblaming . . . $350
Sanitary care: minimal care and disaffection of remains.
We service our families . . . .
 (Isn't that what the bull does to the cow?)

~ § ~

It was a mystery to the Alberto-Culver Company, maker of Alberto VO5 and other personal care products, as well as "Static Guard"—the enemy of static cling. Why were sales to funeral homes of the anti-static product rising so dramatically?

As reported in the *Wall Street Journal,* August Fiebig, the company's director of applied research and patent-holder on "Static Guard," phoned around and learned that funeral directors were using the aerosol spray to secure the fabric lining in caskets—the sheer fabric apparently sometimes has an eerie tendency to shift around as mourners approach.

"They wanted to stop scaring people," said Fiebig.

~ I Died Laughing ~

All I said was "Over my dead body."

It was a beautiful winter day in Salt Lake City. The snow was lightly falling, and it was very cold. I thought it was an appropriate day for the funeral of a lady who was 101 years old.

Her funeral was to be held in one of the older funeral homes in our city, and I was to sing "A Perfect Day." The funeral home was heated with steam heat and had those neat old radiators in each room. The casket had been placed in front of one of them— the conventional spot in the room for the viewing and funeral.

A ways into the funeral, the radiator began to clank as they tend to do. Oddly, it sounded as if it were coming from the casket. Most Utahns were accustomed to the sound and knew what it was. Some chuckled at the coincidence. Then the clanking ceased. I noticed a little blonde blue-eyed boy whispering feverishly into his mother's ear.

A speaker and a song later, the clanking began again. The little boy's eyes got big, and he cried out, "No, Mommy, she is! She's trying to get out!"

Well, that brought the house down. The funeral for this lovely 101-year-old lady ended on a note of humor.

—*Walter Boyden*

She was a town-and-country soprano of the kind often used for augmenting grief at a funeral.

—George Ade

Undertakers have found a new way to get rich. They're mixing Viagra with embalming fluid to raise the dead.

~ § ~

There will be sex after death; we just won't be able to feel it.

—Lily Tomlin

~ § ~

There was a great loss recently in the entertainment world. The man who wrote the song "Hokey Pokey" died. What was really horrible is that they had trouble keeping the body in the casket. They'd put his left leg in, and . . .

~ I Died Laughing ~

I had chosen to do some cleanup in my office at the ad agency that Wednesday morning, so I was wearing Levis and a plaid sport shirt. The secretary at one of the mortuaries called me, frantic. "We were supposed to get a soloist for the Mickelsen service, and we forgot. The family is furious. Can you help?"

The funeral service was in 15 minutes. I was close enough to get to the service, but I had no clothes to change into. I said I would come, but they would have to take me the way I was. The secretary said, "Just come. We'll figure something out."

When I got there, the morticians had gone downstairs to the embalming room, borrowed a suit, shirt, and tie from a dead man, and wanted ME to put it on. The suit would have fit Atilla the Hun. I looked ridiculous, but I went to the Mickelsen funeral and sang "Now is the Hour" while my good friend who accompanied me on the piano giggled. Mr. Mickelsen was laid to rest, and there was a naked dead man downstairs.

—*Walter Boyden*

~ § ~

Why is it we rejoice at a birth and grieve at a funeral?

—*Mark Twain*

~ § ~

It became evident ten minutes into Frank's funeral that he was a bounder. Nobody who spoke could think of a good thing to say about him. One man hemmed and hawed and skirted the issue, and a lady talked about other members of the family.

Finally, the last speaker brought forth the real truth. He said, "Frank did a lot of things wrong in his life but he won't be doing them any more."

—*Walter Boyden*

~ I Died Laughing ~

Three men were killed in an auto accident and arrived at the Pearly Gates. St. Peter lined them up for an interview. He asked each one individually, "If you looked up at your loved ones while lying in your casket, what one thing would you like to hear them say?"

Mr. A: "I'd like to hear them say 'He was such a kind doctor, so gentle and friendly. I wish he was back with us'."

Mr. B: "I'd like to hear them say 'Although he worked for the I.R.S., he was a very helpful honest person and showed me how to get money back'."

Mr. C: "I'd like to hear them say 'My gosh, look! He's moving'! "

I'll put in a good word for you.

From the price list of an enterprising funeral home in Maine:

Caskets . . . . $600 to $INFINITY

~ § ~

In 1678, the funeral bill for a Hartford, Connecticut man who drowned listed the following:
For those who dived for him
  1 Pint of Bushmills
For those who brought him home
  1 Quart of Bushmills
To jury of inquest
  2 Quarts of wine
  1 Gallon hard cider
For funeral
  8 Gallons and 3 qts. of wine
  1 Coffin, 1 windeing sheet
  Barrel of cider

(Cost in today's dollars— about $1,100)

—*Unearthed by Jay Kirk*

Putting the "Fun" Back in Funerals

- Keep singing when everyone else stops.
- Tell the undertaker that he can't close the coffin until you find your contact lens.
- Punch the body and tell people that he hit you first.
- Ask someone to take a picture of you shaking hands with the deceased.
- Walk around telling people you've seen the will and that they are not in it.
- At the cemetery, play taps on a kazoo.
- Tell everyone you don't know that you've been released on "special parole" for this occasion.
- Tell the undertaker your dog just died and ask if he can sneak him into the coffin.
- Slip a whoopee cushion under the seat of the widow.
- Repeatedly ask when the reception will start.
- Brag loudly that you were the deceased's Viagra connection.
- Ask everyone you can find if this really is the "Martin" funeral.
- Give the "thumbs-up" sign as mourners file past.
- Wear hunting clothes and tell people you're waiting for the 21-gun salute.
- Show up at the funeral service in a clown suit.
- Toss a handful of cooked rice onto the deceased and scream "Maggots! Maggots!" and pretend to faint.
- At the cemetery, take bets on how long it takes a body to decompose.
- Promise the minister $100 if he doesn't keep a straight face while praising the deceased.

—From various lists posted on the Internet

But Seriously . . .

In a recent industry journal, the president of the International Cemetery and Funeral Association, who favors pre-need funeral sales, made an astonishing admission: "[T]he at-need transaction puts the customer at a severe disadvantage relative to the funeral director." He cites "well documented problems associated with 'preying on the bereaved' in the at-need situation." Of course, uninformed pre-need buyers are at risk as well.

The average cost of a U.S. funeral in 1999 was nearly $5,000 not counting cemetery and monument expenses. Yet more than half of all widows are living on $10,000 a year or less.

Educated funeral consumers get more for their funeral dollars and usually spend less. However, according to a 1995 study, almost 90% of consumers didn't shop around for a funeral home. Other survey findings:

- 45% used a funeral home that served the family in the past. If it's the one Mom called when Dad died, it's the one you're likely to call when Mom dies.

- 33% called the nearest funeral home, which in some cases may have been the only one in town.

- 11% picked a funeral home based on ethnic or religious affiliation.

That's beginning to change, now that consumers are learning that there can be a BIG difference in price from one funeral home to the next.

The Federal Trade Commission protects your rights as a funeral shopper. Its Funeral Rule provides that:

- funeral homes must give you a General Price List to keep and must show you a casket and vault price list PRIOR to your making any selections

- funeral homes must disclose in writing certain consumer rights

- funeral homes may not require you to purchase more than is wanted, and

- funeral staff may not lie to you—about state laws, among other things.

The General Price List is a menu of goods and services from which you may choose only what you want. *Take the time to read it.* Ask the funeral director to leave the room, or get up and leave yourself if you need to.

A "funeral" is with the casket present. A "memorial service" is without the casket.

One advantage of choosing a memorial service is that it can be scheduled at the convenience of others, perhaps weeks after death. It may be formal or informal and can be held anywhere—at home, in a church, in a public garden, or at the cemetery, for example.

Some people will want to use a nearby funeral home for convenience, regardless of the price. But if you are not using the funeral home facilities for a viewing or the service—perhaps you've picked a simple cremation, for example—then it doesn't matter if you use a less expensive out-of-town funeral home to pick up the body.

In most states it is legal for families or church groups to care for their own dead. Those who have done so have found it a meaningful experience. One pediatric hospice nurse says there is a dramatic improvement in the healing from grief when parents have had a hands-on funeral experience. The following states are the only ones that do not permit families to care for their own dead:

Connecticut   Nebraska
Indiana   New York
Louisiana

The laws in each of these states are contradictory and begging for a court challenge. Of course, you could help to change the laws.

Even if you aren't interested in a do-it-yourself funeral, there are lots of things you can do to take control of the decisions and to personalize the funeral experience:

• build a casket
• bathe and dress the body
• write the obituary
• write a tribute to read at the services
• collect a scrapbook or video of memorabilia
• hold the services in a place that had special meaning, maybe even at the local bowling alley or art gallery if there is no religious affiliation.

The only ways to make your body last "forever" are unusual and very expensive, including mummification or freeze-drying. Funeral-type embalming delays decomposition for only a short term. It is done primarily for cosmetic purposes and costs about $350 to $550. There is no public health purpose served by embalming.

Most funeral directors choose not to be embalmed when making their own funeral plans, according to an industry newsletter. They prefer cremation instead. If you want to know what's involved in embalming, order a video that shows the process: 800-765-0107.

Embalming is not required in any state during the first 24 hours. After that, the following states require either embalming or refrigeration. (Refrigeration is not an alternative in Alaska, Minnesota, or North Dakota.)

Alaska
Arizona (or 48 hours if
    being cremated)
Colorado
Delaware
Florida
Hawaii (after 30 hours)
Idaho
Kansas (extension possible)
Michigan (after 48 hours)
Minnesota (after 72 hours)
Mississippi (24-48 hours)

Missouri
Montana (after 48 hours)
Nevada (may not be required
    for 72 hours)
New Jersey (after 48 hours)
New Mexico
North Dakota (24-48 hours)
Oregon
Pennsylvania
Rhode Island (after 48 hours)
South Dakota
Washington

Temperature has a significant effect on the rate of decomposition. At 70 degrees or less, you can usually keep a body for a day or two after death without embalming.

Embalming is required when moving a body across state lines from Alabama, Alaska, or New Jersey. When shipped via common carrier (i.e., plane) from Kansas, Idaho, and Minnesota, the body must be embalmed.

Private family viewing without embalming is one way to have "good-bye" time and may cost considerably less. Or plan your private family time *before* you ask the funeral director to pick up the body.

A "viewing" is with an open casket. A "visitation" is with a closed casket. If you are planning a visitation, consider one with no casket/body at all. Then hold it at the social hall of the church or even at home—at considerably less expense.

When planning a viewing or visitation, consider having it for one hour just prior to the service. The cost usually will be less, and many elderly people appreciate coming out only once.

Sealer or "protective" caskets do not preserve a body forever. In fact, in a warm climate, a sealer casket speeds decomposition because of the anaerobic bacteria, and the casket is likely to rust out from the inside.

Oprah once did a show on expensive weddings. A year later, no one she interviewed remembered the fancy dresses or elaborate flower arrangements. At funerals, too, it will be the personal stories that people remember, not the expensive casket or flowers you bought. If you want to show someone how much you love them by how much you spend on them, do it while he or she is still alive to appreciate it.

In some states, the medical examiner or coroner is elected and may be a funeral director. Do not feel obligated to use a funeral home you didn't pick. The body can be easily moved to another place of business at no or minimal cost.

When death occurs in one state but services and burial will be in another, it is usually less expensive to work through the receiving funeral home. That funeral home will call a shipping service to pick up the body—for a great deal less than what you might otherwise pay.

Bereavement airfares may *not* be lower than regular discounted fares. Ask about the "cheapest" airfares first, or check the Internet travel sites. Then see what's available for bereavement options. If you choose a bereavement fare, you will need to provide the name of the deceased and the funeral home.

Deep Down,
They're Really Nice People

The only difference between a rut and a grave is the depth.

~ § ~

Forest Lawn is like a Disneyland for shut-ins.

—*Jack Paar*

~ § ~

[From a weekly newspaper:] The poem published this week was composed by an esteemed friend who has lain in his grave for many years for his own amusement.

~ *I Died Laughing* ~

[In a Tennessee cemetery:] She lived a life of virtue and died of cholera morbus caused by eating green fruit in the full hope of a blessed immortality at the early age of 21 years, 7 months. Reader, go thou and do likewise.

~ § ~

When I die, my epitaph or whatever you call those signs on gravestones is going to read: "I joked about every prominent man of my time, but I never met a man I didn't like." I am so proud of that I can hardly wait to die so it can be carved. And when you come to my grave you will find me sitting there, proudly reading it.

—*Will Rogers*

~ § ~

[From a news article:] The incumbent mayor exhumed confidence before the polls closed.

~ § ~

[In a Pennsylvania cemetery:] Persons are prohibited from picking flowers from any but their own graves.

~ § ~

He was a member of Alcoholics Anonymous, Gamblers Anonymous, and Overeaters Anonymous. So I'm having him buried in an unmarked grave.

~ § ~

Unable to attend his father's funeral, a son called his brother and said "Do something nice for Dad and send me the bill." Later, he got a bill for $200 and paid it. The next month another $200 bill came, and he paid it too. But the $200 bills kept coming every month, so he called his brother and asked what was happening. "Well," the brother said, "You said to do something nice for Dad, so I rented him a tuxedo."

Big Deal! I'm used to dust.
—Epitaph requested by *Erma Bombeck*

~ § ~

**In a cemetery office: Rest in Peace . . . until we meet again.
(And then watch out?)**

~ § ~

**Here lies the body of Marion Spen
She gave to worms what she saved from men.**

A bus full of politicians was speeding down a country road when it swerved into a field and crashed into a tree. The farmer who owned the field went over to investigate. Then he dug a hole and buried the politicians.

A few days later, the sheriff drove by and saw the overturned bus. He knocked on the farmhouse door and asked where all the politicians had gone. The farmer said he had buried them.

"They were all dead?" the sheriff asked.

"Well, some of them said they weren't," replied the farmer. "But you know how politicians lie."

Just as we always feared.

Widow: Why is this lot $600 more?
Cemetery man: Better view.

~ § ~

On the tombstone of bigamist Brigham Young:
A man of much encouragement and superb equipment

~ § ~

One fella *asked* to be buried face down—so he can see where he's going. And on his tombstone: "Get off my back."

My sister has a social conscience now. She still wears her fur coat, but across the back she's embroidered a sampler that says "Rest in Peace."
—*Julia Willis*

~ § ~

My wife had just gotten home from work. She is a nurse and works in a hospital. The phone rings, and the guy was trying to sell cemetery lots. My wife interrupted him and asked how soon could he have one ready because it had been a hard day. The guy got upset and told her this was not something to kid about.
—*From an e-mail to the FCA office*

~ § ~

My mother died some years ago. One magazine continued to arrive with increasingly urgent messages: "Soon you will receive no further issues. Please let us know why you no longer want to subscribe." My answer: "Because the subscriber is dead."
The next month, I received a notice saying: "Please send us your new address." I returned the notice with my mother's new address: "_____ Cemetery" complete with street, town, zip code, lot and plot location.
—*Letter to Ann Landers*

~ § ~

Posterity will ne'er survey
A nobler grave than this
Here lie the bones of Castlereagh
Stop, traveler, and piss.

—*Byron*

~ § ~

Every man should have a fair-sized cemetery in which to bury the faults of his friends.
—*Henry Ward Beecher*

Nature's Sextons

The American Burying Beetle, *Nicrophorus americanus,* is now found in only six states. It is also referred to as a carrion beetle or sexton beetle. The burying beetle was placed on the endangered species list in 1989. These one-and-a-half-inch beetles are an important part of a vast host of scavengers that are responsible for recycling decaying materials back into the ecosystem, but a change in habitat is likely to have contributed to their decline.

Using their sense of smell on the antennae, burying beetles can find a dead mouse within an hour of death and from as far away as two miles. A male and female pair go under the body, turn over onto their backs, and experimentally lift the carcass.

It remains unknown how a pair of beetles can "agree" on a burial site or how they are able to keep the carcass moving uniformly in one direction until they find the proper soft ground, usually within a few feet. The soil at the burial site is then loosened by "plowing " through it. Immediate nocturnal burial is important because it prevents flies, active during the day, from laying eggs on the remains.

After burial, the beetles strip away fur or feathers and work the mass into a compact ball. They will then "embalm" it with secretions to preserve the carrion and modify the course of decomposition. The female constructs a short chamber above the carrion in which she lays from 10 to 30 eggs. Larvae hatch within a few days and receive parental care during the entire time they are feeding and growing. This is an extremely rare and highly developed behavior in insects.

The adults continually tend the carcass, removing fungi and covering the carrion ball with an antibacterial secretion. After about a week, the larvae have consumed all but the bones of the carcass, and the adults fly away.

Adapted from an on-line report by Brett Ratcliffe, Ph.D., University of Nebraska

I was to sing for Mrs. Anderson's funeral and asked a friend to accompany me. We were on our lunch hour. As we left, the funeral procession began to form. The parking lot of the funeral home entered onto quite a busy street. The funeral coach and the family car turned right to go to the cemetery. We turned left.

When we had nearly reached our destination, I glanced in my rear view mirror. Much to my horror I realized that the funeral procession had followed us to Taco Bell. I leapt from the car and gave directions to the cemetery to the car just behind.

—Walter Boyden

~ § ~

An old man and woman were married for years, even though they hated each other. More than once the neighbors heard the old man say, "When I die, I will dig my way up and out of the grave to come back to haunt you." They believed he practiced black magic and was responsible for missing cats and dogs.

He died abruptly under strange circumstances, and the funeral had a closed casket. After the burial, the wife went straight to the local bar and began to party. The gaiety of her actions was so extreme, that one of her neighbors finally asked, "Aren't you afraid? That old man said he would dig his way up and out of the grave to come back and haunt you for the rest of your life."

The wife put down her drink and said, "Let the old goat dig. I had him buried upside down."

~ § ~

In the cemetery of Wainscott, Long Island, New York, you will find a man and his wife under identical stones. On her stone is "Rest in Peace," while his stone reads "No Comment."

We Buried Aunt Edna in the Floodplain
by Brent Holmes

We stood there in the pourin' rain
Wishin' we hadn't buried Aunt Edna in the floodplain
But that was where she wanted to be
Out 'tween Uncle Lester and that ol' willow tree

I swear we done what we thought we oughter
But then the river rose up and put 'em both under water
And that river kept rollin' and washin' dirt away
And Edna and Lester come up out of their graves

Them watertight caskets buried down deep
Exploded to the surface 'n then started to creep
Out t'wards the main channel where the river runs fast
And the departed departed 'mongst the carp 'n the bass

But then the dead rose again and continued to float
I yelled, "Big'un, run yonder and fetch us the boat!"
And we follered them caskets a-prayin' and a-hopin'
They didn't run into somethin', bust loose and come open

Aunt Edna couldn't swim even when she was alive
And if that casket'd come open there's no way she'd survived
The current was swift and the current was strong
But we chased them two caskets purt 'near the night long

We caught up with Edna up under a ridge
And lassoed Uncle Lester by a log 'neath a bridge
We tied up them caskets and we towed 'em to town
And we buried 'em both way up on dry ground

I know they's both Christians, they's washed in the blood
And if they ever rise again, it won't be from no flood

On the outskirts of town, there was a big old pecan tree by the cemetery fence. One day two boys filled up a bucketful of nuts and sat down behind the tree, out of sight, and began dividing the nuts. "One for you, one for me. One for you, one for me," said one boy. Several were dropped and rolled toward the fence.

Another boy came riding along the road on his bicycle. As he passed, he thought he heard voices from inside the cemetery. He slowed down to investigate. Sure enough, he heard, "One for you, one for me. One for you, one for me." He just knew what it was. "Oh my," he shuddered. "It's Satan and the Lord dividing the souls at the cemetery."

He jumped back on his bike and rode off. Just around the bend he met an old man with a cane, hobbling along. "Come here quick," said the boy. "You won't believe what I heard. Satan and the Lord are down at the cemetery dividing up the souls."

The man said, "Beat it, kid, can't you see it's hard for me to walk?" When the boy insisted, though, the man hobbled to the cemetery. Standing by the fence they heard, "One for you, one for me. One for you, one for me."

The old man whispered, "Boy, you've been tellin' the truth. Let's see if we can see the devil himself." Shaking with fear, they peered through the fence, yet were still unable to see anything. The old man and the boy gripped the wrought iron bars of the fence tighter and tighter as they tried to get a glimpse of Satan.

At last they heard, "One for you, one for me. And one last one for you. That's all. Now let's go get those nuts by the fence, and we'll be done."

They say the old guy made it back to town five minutes.

But Seriously . . .

There is NO state law that requires a coffin vault in any state. Cemetery regulations, however, may require the use of one—to keep the grave from caving in and minimize maintenance. In that case, a grave liner performs the same function as a coffin vault, at a lower cost.

It is a violation of the Sherman Anti-Trust Act for a cemetery to require you to purchase a vault or marker from the cemetery or to penalize you with a hefty fee for buying one elsewhere.

Sealer caskets and sealer vaults are likely to pop out of the ground during floods. If you want to stay buried, get a cheap one that leaks.

In England, in South Carolina, and perhaps a few other places, folks have started "green burial grounds." Actually, Jewish and Muslim cemeteries qualify, too—no embalming, no metal caskets, no vaults—just a natural return to the earth.

Home body burial may be permissible if you own land in a rural area. Draw a map of the land showing where the family burial grounds will be and ask to have it recorded with the deed. (In a few states, this must be documented by a survey.) If there are no state laws, a good practice is to place it at least 150 feet from a water supply and 50 feet from any power lines that might get buried in the future. Make sure that there are at least two or three feet of earth on top of each casket buried.

In a Blaze of Glory

The mother-in-law called her daughter-in-law and said, "I've decided I want to be cremated."

"Great," replied the daughter-in law. "Get your coat on. I'll be right over."

~ § ~

I'm going out in a blaze of glory.

—*Zadock Smith*

~ *I Died Laughing* ~

We're all cremated equal.

—*Jane Ace*

~ § ~

I was asked to sing "Smoke Gets in Your Eyes" at the service. It was Mr. Allen's favorite song. Why did the people laugh? Mr. Allen was to be cremated.

—*Walter Boyden*

~ § ~

A caller inquiring about the price of cremation: "Does it include the urinal?"

~ § ~

"What a day! I had to take my mother-in-law to the crematory."
"Really rough day, eh?"
"Yeah, she didn't want to go."

—*attributed to Joan Rivers*

~ § ~

My younger brother asked me what happens after we die. I told him we got buried under a bunch of dirt, and worms eat our bodies. I guess I should have told him the truth—that most of us go to hell and burn eternally, but I didn't want to upset him.

~ § ~

Make an ash of yourself.

—*Mabel Lepper*

But Seriously . . .

At this writing, the national cremation rate is almost 25%. By 2010, it is likely to be 40%. In many areas of the West Coast, it is already 50% or more. A majority of funeral directors opt for cremation themselves, according to an article in the *Funeral Monitor.*

Because more people are choosing simple cremation rather than a one-of-everything funeral, the industry is coming up with new ways to drive up the costs. "Identification viewing" sounds very official but appears to be one such ploy. After all, the funeral home is supposed to know whose body it is when they pick it up. Some are charging for identification viewing or asking you to bring mother's clothes and charging for "preparation" for ID viewing. Or hinting that you won't want to see Mother's body in a cardboard box, so surely you'll want one of their nicer cremation containers. You can decline any such charges.

The materials left after the cremation process have mistakenly been called "ashes." In reality, they're bone fragments—more like broken seashells—that are usually pulverized. A better term is "cremated remains."

Cremated remains may be kept in your home, under the laws of every state. There are no "cremains police" checking up to see if they're still there. There are many options for what you can do with cremated remains:

- Bury them in a cemetery lot, or above ground in a columbarium niche, or in a cemetery's scattering garden. If there are two family members buried in different locations and you'd like to be next to both, you can instruct your family to divide the cremated remains.

- Scatter or bury them on private land, with the land-owner's permission.
- Scatter them in the ocean. (Off the coast of California, this must be at least 500 yards from shore, and not dropped or flung from the Golden Gate Bridge.)
- Divide them among family and friends; special lockets are even sold for this purpose.

An urn is not required for cremated remains. You can keep them in the plain box that comes from the crematory. Or you can purchase a container of your own. One lady put her grandmother's "ashes" in a cookie jar.

There is no safety or maintenance purpose served by using an urn vault, although the cemetery may try to crank up its bill by suggesting that you need one. You have a right to decline that purchase if you so choose.

From *Les Urnes Utiles,* © 1983 by Edward Gorey

The Great Perhaps

I go and seek the great Perhaps.

—Rabelais

~ § ~

My dear old Dad left this world two years ago. He was one fine accountant and not given to unnecessary expenditures. Dad negotiated and bought his own funeral. He was cremated and the cremains were to be placed in the family plot. They tried to get me to buy an urn for the cremains in the cemetery. I told them it wasn't necessary, but if they would keep the UPS sticker on the side of the cardboard box, we might be able to track his afterlife via the UPS site on the Internet.

—FCA member, in an e-mail to the national office

~ § ~

When we talk to God, we're praying. When God talks to us, we're schizophrenic.

—Jane Wagner

~ § ~

On being urged to see a priest: "No, I am curious to see what happens in the next world to those who die unshriven."

—Perugino

~ § ~

The chief problem about death is the fear that there may be no afterlife—a depressing thought, particularly for those who have bothered to shave. Also, there is the fear that there is an afterlife, but no one will know where it is being held.

—Woody Allen

I desire to go to hell and not heaven. In the former place I shall enjoy the company of popes, kings, and princes, while in the latter are only beggars, monks, and apostles. —*Machiavelli*

~ § ~

A saint is a dead sinner revised and edited.
—*Ambrose Bierce*

~ § ~

"Doctor, do you believe in Spiritualism?"
"Naturally not. What would become of me if the dead should return?" —*From Bless Thee, Bully Doctor*

The Resurrection of a Rabbit
by Brent Holmes

Our cat drug up a rabbit it had killed
It does that now and then
Eunice said, "Handsome! That's the neighbor's rabbit!
It must've gotten out of its pen!"

And before I could say, "What'er we gonna do?"
Eunice took that rabbit to the sink
And started shampooin' that stiff bunny's fur
She said, "They've gone out of town, I think"

She said, "If we can clean it up and git it back in its pen
Before they get home we'll be fine"
Then she said, "Git my blow dryer so I can fluff him up"
I thought she'd done lost her mind

But we fluffed him up nice and put him back in his pen
So he'd look like he died in his sleep
And the neighbors came home and didn't say nothin'
But when we saw 'em at the end of the week

They said, "The strangest thing happened while we were gone"
Eunice and I tried not to grin
They said, "We buried our rabbit before we left town
When we got home he was back in his pen!"

(From *The Road Less Graveled*, © 1997 by Brent Holmes)

~ § ~

When I reflect upon the number of disagreeable people who I
know have gone to a better world, I am moved to lead a different
life.

—Mark Twain

There are many canonized on earth that shall never be saints in Heaven. —*Sir Thomas Brown*

~ § ~

An atheist is a man who has no invisible means of support. —*John Buchan*

~ § ~

An apology for the devil: It must be remembered that we have heard only one side of the case; God has written all the books. —*Samuel Butler*

~ § ~

To follow you, I'm not content.
How do I know which way you went?

Copyright © WhiteLight Art Caskets

His was the sort of career that made the Recording Angel think seriously about taking up shorthand. —*Bentley*

~ § ~

On his deathbed and asked by his clergyman to repudiate the devil, "This is no time for making enemies." —*attributed to several famous people*

If all else fails, immortality can always be assured by spectacular error.

—*John Kenneth Galbraith*

~ § ~

Here lies an atheist
All dressed up
And no place to go

A Cuban chief, exhorted to change his faith by Spaniards: "I thank my gods that I am going, as you say, to hell, for there I shall, at any rate, meet no Christians."

—*From Famous Last Words*

~ § ~

Thoreau was asked on his deathbed if he'd made his peace with God. To which he replied, "I wasn't aware we'd quarreled."

~ I Died Laughing ~

Wilson Mizner on his deathbed talking to his priest:
"Why should I talk to you? I've just been talking to your boss."

~ § ~

An Illinois man left the snow-filled streets of Chicago for a vacation in Florida. His wife was on a business trip and was planning to meet him there the next day. When he reached his hotel, he decided to send his wife a quick romantic e-mail.

Unable to find the scrap of paper on which he had written her new e-mail address, he typed it in from memory. Unfortunately, he missed one letter, and his note was directed instead to an elderly preacher's wife whose husband had passed away only the day before.

When the grieving widow checked her e-mail, she took one look at the monitor, let out a piercing scream and fell to the floor in a dead faint. Her family rushed into the room and saw the message on the screen:

DEAREST WIFE:
JUST GOT CHECKED IN. EVERYTHING PREPARED FOR
YOUR ARRIVAL TOMORROW.
ETERNALLY YOURS.
P.S. SURE IS HOT DOWN HERE.

~ § ~

Life is like a cow pasture. If you walk through it with your head down, you'll avoid the crap but never find the gate.

~ § ~

The more you complain, the longer God lets you live.

~ I Died Laughing ~

On their way to a justice of the peace to get married, a couple had a fatal car accident. The couple found themselves sitting outside the Pearly Gates waiting for St. Peter to do an intake. St. Peter finally showed up, and they asked if they could possibly get married in heaven.

"I don't know. This is the first time anyone has asked. Let me go find out." The couple waited and waited . . . for months.

"Yes," said a bedraggled St. Peter when he returned. "You can get married in heaven."

"Great," said the couple. "But what if things don't work out? Could we also get a divorce in heaven?"

Red-faced, St. Peter slammed down his clipboard. "Come on," he shouted. "It took me three months to find a priest up here! Do you have any idea how long it will take me to find a lawyer?"

~ § ~

When the widow got to heaven, she started looking around for her husband. "What was your husband's name?" asked St. Peter.

"John Smith," replied the widow.

"We have a lot of Smiths here. What do you remember most about your husband?"

She thought for a minute, then replied, "He always used to say that if I ever were unfaithful, he'd turn over in his grave."

"Oh, you mean Pinwheel!"

"When you die, are you ever allowed to come back?"
"Only if you had your hand stamped."   —*Peanuts*

~ § ~

Heinrich Heine, on his deathbed: "God will pardon me. It's his profession."

The man had just arrived in heaven, and St. Peter said he would show him around. As they passed one large gathering, St. Peter whispered, "Those are the Muslims." They went on a little farther and passed another group having a grand time. St. Peter whispered, "Those are the Catholics." And again, St. Peter whispered as they passed the next group, "Those are the Jews."

Strolling farther down the grassy path, the man finally asked, "Why did you keep whispering back there?"

"Because they think they're here all alone."

.....384 F. Gone Over the Big Divide.

Reincarnation
by Wallace McRae

"What does reincarnation mean?"
a cowpoke ast his friend.
His pal replied, "It happens when
Yer life has reached its end.

They comb yer hair, and warsh yer neck,
and clean yer fingernails,
And lay you in a padded box
Away from life's travails.

The box and you goes in a hole,
That's been dug into the ground.
Reincarnation starts in when
Yore planted 'neath a mound.

Them clods melts down, just like yer box,
And you who is inside.
And then yore just beginnin' on
Yer transformation ride.

In a while the grass'll grow
Upon your rendered mound.
Till some day, on yer moldered grave
A lonely flower is found.

And say a hoss should wander by
And graze upon that flower
That once wuz you, but now's become
Yer vegetative bower.

~ *I Died Laughing* ~

The posey that the hoss done ate,
Up, with his other feed,
Makes bone and fat and muscle
Essential to the steed.

But some is left that he can't use
And so it passes through,
And finally lays upon the ground,
This thing, that once wuz you.

Then say, by chance, I wanders by
And sees this upon the ground,
And I ponders, and I wonders at,
This object that I found.

I thinks about reincarnation,
Of life, and death, and such,
And come away concludin': Slim,
'You ain't changed, all that much'."

(From **Cowboy Curmudgeon and Other Poems**, © 1992 By Wallace McRae)

~ § ~

My Garden Rock

But Seriously . . .

Although some clergy conduct funerals free of charge as a part of their pastoral commitment, many expect an honorarium for presiding at a service.

Because families may overlook this obligation in the emotions of the moment, the mortician may offer to handle the payment for you. However, one Chicago woman was told by the funeral director to put $300 cash in a plain white envelope for the priest. In checking with the diocese later, the woman learned that $175 was "expected."

There are ways to live on—through organ or body donation.

More than 60,000 people are waiting for organ transplants, and 20,000 die each year because they didn't get a needed organ. Even the elderly can donate their eyes. Have you talked about this with your family? Do they know what your wishes are? Will they know enough to make the offer before the hospital has to ask?

Some of us would rather have doctors practice on us when we're dead than when we're alive. Body donation to a medical school for study or research may also reduce your funeral expenses, if the medical school pays for transportation. And you can consider it just a loan. After medical study, the body is usually cremated. The cremated remains can be returned to the family for final disposition, but be sure the college knows your wishes at the time of donation.

Locks of Love accepts donation of hair ten inches or longer—any color—to make wigs for children who have lost hair because of medical treatment or other medical causes. Gray hair is sold to help fund the manufacturing of these wigs, so even us old folks can help. Be sure to check the donation requirements and procedures.

Locks of Love
1640 S. Congress Ave., Ste. 104
Palm Springs, FL 33461
561-963-1677 or 888-896-1588

In addition to recycling your body or body parts, take an inventory of your medical devices, such as pacemakers, glasses, hearing aids, insulin pumps, walkers, etc. They can be recycled too, and there is an urgent need for them in many poor countries.

For pacemakers, contact:
Heart to Heart
220 34th St. W.
Billings, MT 59102
406-656-7687

For hearing aids:
Hear Now
9745 E. Hamden Ave Ste 300
Denver, CO 80231
800-648-HEAR

For glasses, check a local Lions Club. For international donation of glasses:
OEU
4 Parkdale Crescent NW
Calgary, AB T2N 3T8
Canada

For other items, check with your doctor, your hospital social worker, or the visiting nurses association.

A Dying Person's Bill of Rights

I have the right to be treated as a living human being until I die.

I have the right to be cared for by those who can maintain a sense of hopefulness, however changing this may be.

I have the right to express my feelings and emotions about my approaching death in my own way.

I have the right to expect others to listen.

I have the right to participate in decisions concerning my care and the way I wish to live and die.

I have the right to expect continuing medical and nursing attention even though "cure" goals must be changed to "comfort" goals.

I have the right to be free from pain.

I have the right not to be deceived.

I have the right to have my questions answered honestly.

I have the right to have help from and for my family in accepting my death.

I have the right to retain my individuality and not be judged for my decisions which may be contrary to others.

I have the right to discuss and enlarge my religious and/or spiritual experiences, whatever these may mean to others.

I have the right to be cared for by caring, sensitive, knowledgeable people who will attempt to understand my needs and will be able to gain some satisfaction in helping me face my death.

I have the right not to die alone, though I may choose to be alone.

I have the right to die in peace and dignity.

Passed out in a class on Death & Dying, but there was no credit to the writer. If you know the origins of this fine piece, please let me know so I can add the author in the next printing.

Funeral Consumers Alliance

Funeral Consumers Alliance

Nationwide there are more than 120 funeral consumer information societies and alliances. All are nonsectarian nonprofit organizations, and most are run by volunteers. The active groups do an annual price survey of area funeral homes. Some have negotiated a discount for members at certain cooperating funeral homes—sort of a cooperative buyers club. All have end-of-life and funeral-planning information.

Funeral Consumers Alliance (FCA) is the national organization under which the local groups are affiliated. FCA maintains a Web site at <http://www.funerals.org>. If there is no local group in your area and you would like to help start one, please contact the FCA office at 800-765-0107. You may ask for general information, too.

Because many of these groups are run by volunteers, the phone numbers listed below may have changed by the time you're reading this. If you have difficulty reaching an organization, check with the FCA office.

Alabama
Call the FCA office

Alaska
Anchorage Cook Inlet Memorial Society
P.O. Box 102414, 99510
907-566-3732

Arizona
Phoenix Valley Memorial Society
Box 0423, Chandler, 85244-0423
480-929-9659
Prescott Memorial Society of Prescott
P.O. Box 1090, 86302-1090
520-778-3000
Tucson Memorial Society of So. Arizona
P.O. Box 12661, 85732-2661
520-721-0230

Arkansas
Fayetteville NW Arkansas Mem. Society
P.O. Box 3055, 72702-3055
501-582-1631

Little Rock Memorial Society of AR
11621 Hilaro Springs Rd., 72206
501-652-6361 or 888-278-7556

California
Bakersfield Kern Memorial Society
P.O. Box 1202, 93302-1202
661-854-5689 or 661-366-7266
Berkeley Bay Area Funeral Society
P.O. Box 264, 94701-0264
510-841-6653
Cotati Redwood Funeral Society
P.O. Box 7501, 94931-7501
707-568-7684
Eureka/Arcata Humboldt Funeral Society
P.O. Box 856, Arcata 95518
707-822-8599
Fresno Valley Memorial Society
P.O. Box 101, 93707-0101
559-268-2181
Los Angeles Los Angeles Funeral Society
Box 92313, Pasadena, CA 91109
626-683-3545 or 683-3752

Modesto Stanislaus Memorial Society
P.O.Box 4252, 95352-4252
209-521-7690

Palo Alto FCA of San Mateo & Santa Clara
Counties
P.O. Box 60448, 94306-0448
650-321-2109 or 888-775-5553

Sacramento Sacramento Valley Mem. Soc.
P.O. Box 161688, 95816-1688
916-451-4641

San Diego San Diego Memorial Society
4883 Ronson Ct., Ste. L, 92111
858-874-7921

San Luis Obispo Central Coast Mem. Soc.
P.O. Box 679, 93406-0679
805-543-6133

Santa Barbara Funeral Consumers
Alliance~Channel Cities
P.O. Box 1778, Ojai, CA 93024
805-640-0109 or 800-520-PLAN

Santa Cruz FCA of Monterey Bay
Box 2900, 95063-2900
831-426-3308

Stockton FCA of San Joaquin
Box 4832, 95204-4832
209-465-2741

Colorado

Denver Funeral Consumer Society of CO
4101 E. Hampden Ave., 80222
303-759-2800 or 888-438-6431

Connecticut

Bridgewater Fun'l Consumer Soc of CT
P.O. Box 34, 06752
860-355-4197 or 800-607-2801

Delaware

Served by Funeral Consumers Alliance of
Maryland

District of Columbia

Washington Mem Soc of Metro Washington
1500 Harvard St. NW, 20009
202-234-7777

Florida

Cocoa Fun'l Consumers Assn. Brevard Co
P.O. Box 276, 32923-0276
321-242-1421 or 321-255-2100

DeBary Funeral Society of Mid-Florida
P.O. Box 392, 32713-0392
904-789-1682 or 407-668-6822

Deerfield Beach Palm Beach Fun'l Soc.
1626 SE 3rd Ct., Ste 144, 33441
954-429-0280 or 888-925-0007

Ft. Myers Funeral & Mem. Soc. of SW Fla.
P.O. Box 7756, 33911-7756
941-573-0507

Gainesville Memorial Soc. of Alachua Co.
Box 14662, 32604-4662
352-337-0460

Orlando FCA Greater Orlando
P.O. Box 953, Goldenrod, FL 32733
407-677-5009

Pensacola & Ft. Walton Beach
Funeral & Memorial Society of W. Fla.
5425 Dynasty Dr., 32504
850-477-9085

Sarasota Funeral Consumers Alliance ~
Sarasota & Manatee Counties
P.O. Box 15833, 34277-5833
941-953-3740

St. Petersburg Suncoast-Tampa Mem Soc
719 Arlington Ave. N., 33701
727-520-8922

Tallahassee Funeral Consumers Assn. of
Leon County
1006 Buena Vista Dr., 32304
850-224-2082

Tampa Funeral Consumers Assn. of
Tampa Bay
18902 Arbor Dr., Lutz, 33549-5051
813- 948-1990

Georgia

Atlanta Memorial Society of Georgia
1911 Cliff Valley Way NE, 30329
404-634-2896 or 800-840-4339

Macon Middle Georgia Chapter
5276 Zebulon Rd., 31210
800-840-4339

Hawaii

Honolulu Memorial Society of Hawaii
505 Ward St., Ste. 203, 96814
808-589-2884

Idaho

Boise Funeral Consumers Alliance of Idaho
P.O. Box 1919, 83701-1919
208-426-0032

Illinois

Chicago Chicago Memorial Association
Box 2923, 60690-2923
773-238-3746

Urbana Champaign Co. Memorial Society
309 W. Green St., 61801

Indiana
Bloomington Bloomington Mem. Soc.
2120 N. Fee Lane, 47408
Indianapolis Indianapolis Memorial Soc.
5805 E. 56th St., 46226
317-844-1371
Valparaiso Memorial Soc. of NW Indiana
P.O. Box 329, 46384-0329
219-464-3024

Iowa
Iowa City Mem. Soc. of Iowa River Valley
120 N. Dubuque St., 52245
319-338-2637
For all other areas, call the FCA office

Kansas
Check Missouri or call the FCA office

Kentucky
Louisville Mem. Soc. of Greater Louisville
P.O. Box 5326, 40255-5326
502-454-4855

Louisiana
Baton Rouge Mem Soc/Grtr Baton Rouge
8470 Goodwood Ave., 70806

Maine
Auburn Memorial Society of Maine
Box 3122, 04212-3122
207-786-4323 or 800-218-9885

Maryland
Bethesda Funeral Consumers Alliance of
Maryland & Environs
9601 Cedar Lane, 20814
800-564-0017

Massachusetts
Boston The Memorial Society
66 Marlborough St., 02116
617-859-7990 or 888-666-7990
East Orleans Funeral Consumers Alliance
of Cape Cod
P. O. Box 1375, 02643-1375
508-862-2522 or 800-976-9552
New Bedford Memorial Soc. of SE Mass.
71 8th St., 02740
508-996-0046
Springfield Mem Soc of Western Mass.
P.O. Box 2821, 01101-2821
413-783-7987

Michigan
Ann Arbor Mem Advisory & Planning Soc.
2030 Chaucer Drive, 48103
734-665-9516

Detroit Greater Detroit Memorial Society
P.O. Box 24054, 48224-4054
313-886-0998
Flint Memorial Society of Flint
P.O. Box 4315, 48504-4315
For all other areas, call the FCA office

Minnesota
St. Cloud Minn. Funeral & Memorial Soc.
717 Riverside Dr. SE, 56304
320-252-7540

Mississippi
Call the FCA office

Missouri
Kansas City Funeral Consumer Alliance
of Greater Kansas City
4501 Walnut St., 64111
816-561-6322

Montana
Billings Memorial Society of Montana
1024 Princeton Ave., 59102
406-252-5065
Missoula Five Valleys Memorial Society
405 University Ave. 59801
406-728-6248

Nebraska
Call the FCA office

Nevada
Reno Funeral Consumer Info. Soc. of NV
Box 8413, Univ. Sta., 89507-8413
775-329-7705

New Hampshire
Epping Memorial Society of N.H.
P.O. Box 941, 03042-0941
603-679-5721

New Jersey
Cherry Hill Memorial Society of So. Jersey
401 Kings Highway N., 08034
856-235-2783
East Brunswick Raritan Valley Mem Soc
176 Tices Ln., 08816
732-572-1470
Lincroft Mem Assoc. of Monmouth County
1475 W. Front St., 07738
732-747-7950

~ I Died Laughing ~

Madison Morris Memorial Society
Box 509, 07940-0509
973-540-9140
Montclair Funeral Consumers Alliance of
Essex Co.
P.O. Box 1327, 07042-1327
973-783-1145
Paramus Central Memorial Society
156 Forest, 07652
201-385-4153
Plainfield Memorial Society of Plainfield
724 Park Ave., 07060
908-889-6289
Princeton Princeton Memorial Association
50 Cherry Hill Road, 08540
609-430-7250

New Mexico
Albuquerque FCA of Northern NM
P.O. Box 53464, 87153
505-296-5902
Las Cruces Mem. & Fun'l Soc of So NM
P.O. Box 6531, 88006-6531
505-526-7761

New York
Albany Mem Soc Hudson-Mohawk Region
405 Washington Ave., 12206-2604
518-465-9664
Binghamton Southern Tier Memorial Soc.
c/o Haesler, 300 Fordham Rd,
Vestal 13850
Buffalo Greater Buffalo Memorial Society
695 Elmwood Ave., 14222-1601
716-837-8636
Corning Memorial Society of Grtr Corning
P.O. Box 23,Painted Post, NY 14870
607-962-7132 or 607-936-6563
Long Island Mem Society of Long Island
P.O. Box 701, Greenlawn, 11740-0701
631-544-0383
Ithaca Ithaca Memorial Society
Box 134, 14851-0134
607-273-8316
New Hartford Mohawk Valley Mem Soc
P. O. Box 322,13413-0322
315-797-2396 or 315-735-6268
Poughkeepsie Mid-Hudson Memorial Soc.
249 Hooker Ave., 12603
914-229-0241
Rochester Rochester Memorial Society
220 Winton Road South, 14610
716-461-1620
Syracuse Syracuse Memorial Society
P.O. Box 67, De Witt, NY 13214
315-446-0557

Yorktown Heights Funeral Consumer Info
Society of Westchester
460 York Ct., 10598-3726
914-285-0585

North Carolina
Asheville Blue Ridge Memorial Society
P.O. Box 2601, 28802-2601
828-669-2587
Chapel Hill Funeral Consumers Alliance
of the Triangle
1507 Doughton St., Raleigh,27608
919-834-6898
Charlotte FCA of Central Carolinas
P.O. Box 26507, 28221
704-596-1208
Wilmington Mem. Soc. of Coastal Carolina
P.O. Box 4262, 28406-4262
910-458-4136

North Dakota
See South Dakota

Ohio
Akron Mem Soc of Akron-Canton Area
3300 Morewood Road, 44333
330-836-4418 or 330-849-1030
Cincinnati Mem. Soc. of Greater Cincinnati
536 Linton St., 45219
513-651-0909
Cleveland Cleveland Memorial Society
21600 Shaker Blvd, Shaker Hgts 44122
216-751-5515
Columbus Mem Soc of Columbus Area
P.O. Box 14835, 43214-4835
614-436-8911
Toledo Memorial Soc of Northwest Ohio
2210 Collingwood Blvd., 43620-1147
419-475-1429

Oklahoma
Ardmore FCA of the SW
1550 Kknox Rd., 73401
800-371-2221

Oregon
Portland Oregon Memorial Association
P.O. Box 25578, 97298
503-297-3513 or 888-475-5520

Pennsylvania
Erie Memorial Society of Erie
Box 3495, 16508-3495
814-4564433
Harrisburg Mem. Soc. of Grtr Harrisburg
1280 Clover Lane, 17113
717-564-8507

94

~ I Died Laughing ~

Philadelphia Mem. Soc. Grtr Philadelphia
1906 Rittenhouse Sq. 19103-5793
215-545-9210
Pittsburgh Pittsburgh Memorial Society
605 Morewood Ave., 15213
412-621-4740
State College Mem. Soc. of Central PA
780 Waupelani Dr. Ext., 16801
814-237-7605

Rhode Island
East Greenwich Memorial Society of R.I.
119 Kenyon Ave., 02818
401-884-1227

South Carolina
Columbia Funeral & Memorial Soc. of SC
2701 Heyward St.,29205
803-772-7054

South Dakota
Lemmon Funeral Consumer Info Soc.
of the Dakotas
HCR 66 Box 10, Lemmon, 57638
605-374-5336

Tennessee
Chattanooga Mem. Soc. of Chattanooga
3224 Navajo Dr., 37411
423-886-3480
Knoxville East Tenn. Memorial Society
P.O. Box 10507, 37939
865-483-4843
Memphis Funeral Consumers Alliance of
Mid-South
P.O. Box 770388, 38177
901-685-2464 or 680-9149
Nashville Funeral Consumers Alliance of
Middle Tennessee
1808 Woodmont Blvd., 37215
615-907-3364 or 888-254-3872

Texas
**Amarillo, El Paso, Lubbock, Rio Grand
Valley** FCA of the Southwest
2875 E. Parker Rd., Plano, TX 75074
800-371-2221
Austin Austin Memorial & Burial Info. Soc.
P.O. Box 4382, 78765-4382
512-480-0555
**Commerce, Dallas, Denton, Fort Worth,
Longview, Tyler** FCA of No. TX
2875 E. Parker Rd., Plano, TX 75074
972-509-5686 or 800-371-2221
Corpus Christi FCA of So. Texas
3125 Horne Rd., 78415
800-371-2221

Houston FCA of the Houston Area
5200 Fannin St., 77004-5899
713-526-4267or 888-282-4267
San Antonio San Antonio Mem. Society
7150 Interstate 10 West, 78213
210-341-2213
Waco FCA N. TX, Central TX Chapter
4209 N. 27th St., 76708-1509
800-371-2221

Utah
Orem Funeral Consumers Alliance of Utah
1823 S 250 E, 84058-7840
801-226-4701

Vermont
East Montpelier Vermont Memorial Society
1630 Clark Rd., 05651
802-476-4300 or 800-805-0007

Virginia
Arlington Memorial Society of No. Virginia
4444 Arlington Blvd., 22204
703-271-9240
Charlottesville Mem. Planning Soc. of
the Piedmont
717 Rugby Road, 22903
804-293- 8179
Virginia Beach Mem. Soc. of Tidewater
P.O. Box 4621, 23454- 4621
757-428- 6900

Washington
Seattle People's Memorial Association
2366 Eastlake Ave. E.
Areis Bldg. #409, 98102
206-325-0489
Spokane Spokane Memorial Association
P.O. Box 13613, 99213-3613
509-924-8400
Yakima Funeral Assoc. Centrl Washington
1916 N. 4th St., 98901
509-248- 4533

West Virginia
Lewisburg Mem. Soc. of Greenbrier Valley
P.O. Box 1277, 24901
Morgantown & NE area: call MD Alliance
800-564-0017

Wisconsin
Milwaukee Funeral Consumer Info. Soc.
13001 W. North Ave., Brookfield, 53005
262-238-0507 or 800-491-8150

Wyoming
Call the FCA office

95

Index